Ingham Surname

Ireland: 1600s to 1900s

From Ireland Church Records of Baptism, Marriage and Death

Comprised of Roman Catholic and Church of Ireland Records

From Counties Carlow, Cork, Kerry and Dublin City

Compiled by **Donovan Hurst**

December 1, 2012

ISBN: 0985696826
ISBN-13: 978-0-9856968-2-5

Dedication

This work is dedicated to all of those that came before us and shaped our lives to make us the people that we are today.

Table of Contents

Introduction

This is a compilation of individuals who have the surname of Ingham that lived in the country of Ireland from the 1600s to the 1900s. I have placed each entry into one of four categories: Families, Individual Births/Baptisms, Individual Burials, and Individual Marriages. If a marriage entry primarily concerns an Individual Ingham who is female, then I have placed that entry under the category of Individual Marriages. If a marriage entry primarily concerns an Individual Ingham who is male, then I have placed that entry under the category of Families. Images of many of these listings are available at http://churchrecords.irishgenealogy.ie/churchrecords/.

To help guide the reader of this work, the format of this book is as follows:

- Main Family Entry (Husband and Wife) (Father and Mother)

  - Child of Main Family Entry, including Spouse(s) when available

    - Grandchild of Main Family Entry, including Spouse(s) when available

      - Great-Grandchild of Main Family Entry, including Spouse(s) when available

(Bolded Text) following any entry includes any additional information such as Residence(s), Occupation(s), Signature(s), etc. when available.

Hurst

Some of the fonts used in this work symbolizes Celtic writing. The traditional letters, numbers, and punctuation marks and their Celtic counterparts are as follows:

Traditional Letters (Uppercase & Lowercase)

A a B b C c D d E f G g H h I i J j K k L l M m N n O o P p Q q R r S s T t U u V v W w X x Y y Z z

Celtic Letters (Uppercase & Lowercase)

A a B b C c D ð E e F ꝼ G g H h I i J j K k L l M m

N n O o P p Q q R ʀ S s T t U u V ʋ W ꞷ X x Y y Z z

Traditional Numbers

1 2 3 4 5 6 7 8 9 10

Celtic Numbers

1 2 3 4 5 6 7 8 9 10

Traditional Punctuation

. , : ' " & - ( )

Celtic Punctuation

. , : ' " & - ( )

Parish Churches
Cork & Ross
(Roman Catholic or RC)

Bantry Parish and Cork - South Parish.

Dublin (Church of Ireland)

Arbour Hill Barracks Parish, Clontarf Parish, St. Anne Parish, St. Audoen Parish, St. Bride Parish, St. Catherine Parish, St. George Parish, St. James Parish, St. John Parish, St. Luke Parish, St. Mark Parish, St. Mary Parish, St. Michan Parish, St. Nicholas Within Parish, St. Nicholas Without Parish, St. Paul Parish, St. Peter Parish, and St. Werburgh Parish.

Dublin (Roman Catholic or RC)

Harrington Street Parish, SS. Michael & John Parish, St. Agatha Parish, St. Andrew Parish, St. Audoen Parish, St. Catherine Parish, St. James Parish, St. Mary Parish, St. Mary, Donnybrook Parish, St. Mary, Haddington Road Parish, St. Mary, Pro Cathedral Parish, St. Michan Parish, and St. Nicholas Parish.

Kerry (Church of Ireland)

Tralee Parish.

Ingham Surname Ireland: 1600s to 1900s

Families

- Albert Edward Ingham & Alice Harriet Ingham

  - Alice Kathleen Harriet Ingham – b. 20 Jan 1898, bapt. 9 Feb 1898 (Baptism, **Arbour Hill Barracks Parish**)

Albert Edward Ingham (father):

Residence - Staff Quarters Royal Barracks - February 9, 1898

Occupation - Bandmaster 2ⁿᵈ R W Kent Regiment - February 9, 1898

- Charles Ingham & Jane Huntington – 19 Oct 1709 (Marriage, **St. Nicholas Without Parish**)

- Charles Ingham & Mary Ingham

  - Dominick Ingham – bapt. 9 Jun 1713 (Baptism, **St. Catherine Parish**)

- Charles David Ingham & Helen Anne Haynes – 12 Feb 1846 (Marriage, **St. Audoen Parish (RC)**)

Signature:

  - John Ingham – bapt. 3 Jan 1847 (Baptism, **St. Mary, Pro Cathedral Parish (RC)**)

  - Mary Ellen Ingham – bapt. 7 Jun 1849 (Baptism, **St. Audoen Parish (RC)**)

  - Susan Mary Ingham – bapt. 7 Dec 1851 (Baptism, **St. Audoen Parish (RC)**)

  - Ellen Christine Ingham – b. 26 Dec 1855, bapt. 26 Dec 1855 (Baptism, **St. Michan Parish (RC)**)

  - Helen Teresa Ingham – b. 23 Oct 1857, bapt. 26 Oct 1857 (Baptism, **St. Audoen Parish (RC)**)

Hurst

o   Charles Patrick Ingham – b. 18 Mar 1859, bapt. 27 Mar 1859 (Baptism, **St. Mary, Pro Cathedral Parish** (RC))

Charles David Ingham (father):

Residence - Dorset Street - December 26, 1855

39 Usher's Quay - October 26, 1857

5 Lower Dominick Street - March 27, 1859

- Daniel Ingham & Susan Ingham

  o   Mary Ingham – bapt. 5 Nov 1730 (Baptism, **St. Catherine Parish**)

- Dennis Ingham & Catherine Casey – 22 Jul 1828 (Marriage, **Bantry Parish** (RC))

  o   Cornelius (C o r n e l i u s) Ingham – bapt. 28 May 1833 (Baptism, **Bantry Parish** (RC))

- Edward Ingham & Elizabeth Unknown

  o   Edward Ingham – bapt. 2 Apr 1785 (Baptism, **St. Werburgh Parish**)

- George Ingham & Mary Mannion

  o   Mary Alice Ingham – b. 14 Mar 1883, bapt. 21 Mar 1883 (Baptism, **St. Michan Parish** (RC))

George Ingham (father):

Residence - 2 Blessington Street - March 21, 1883

- Henry Ingham & Manella Ingham

  o   Henry Ingham – bapt. 5 May 1834 (Baptism, **St. Mary, Pro Cathedral Parish** (RC))

- Hugh John Ingham & Teresa McDonnell – 25 Feb 1873 (Marriage, **St. Mary Parish** (RC))

  o   Mary Ingham – b. 1874, bapt. 1874 (Baptism, **St. Mary Parish** (RC)) o   John Joseph Stanley Ingham – b. 24 Apr 1877, bapt. 4 May 1877 (Baptism, **St. Mary, Haddington Road Parish** (RC))

Hugh John Ingham (father):

Residence - 96 Pembroke Road - May 4, 1877

- James Ingham & Anne Unknown
  - o Agnes Ingham – bapt. 18 Sep 1733 (Baptism, **St. John Parish**)

- John Ingham & Agnes Bradley
  - o Henry John Ingham – b. 3 Nov 1894, bapt. 7 Nov 1894 (Baptism, **St. Mary, Pro Cathedral Parish** (RC))
  - o John Joseph Ingham – b. 17 May 1896, bapt. 20 May 1896 (Baptism, **St. Mary, Pro Cathedral Parish** (RC))
  - o Bernard (B e r n a r d) Ingham – b. 17 Jan 1898, bapt. 21 Jan 1898 (Baptism, **St. Mary, Pro Cathedral Parish** (RC))
  - o Elizabeth Agnes Ingham – b. 21 Aug 1899, bapt. 4 Sep 1899 (Baptism, **St. Mary, Pro Cathedral Parish** (RC))

John Ingham (father):

Residence - 1 Upper Rutland Street - November 7, 1894

May 20, 1896

45 Lower Gloucester Street - January 21, 1898

Rotunda - September 4, 1899

Hurst

- John Ingham & Anne Tinworth

  o Mary Jane Ingham – bapt. 9 Jul 1846 (Baptism, **Bantry Parish (RC)**)

- John Ingham & Anne Unknown

  o John Ingham – bapt. 24 Sep 1780 (Baptism, **St. Catherine Parish**)

John Ingham (father):

Residence - Tripelo - September 24, 1780

- John Ingham & Bridget Ingham, bur. 13 Dec 1652 (Burial, **St. John Parish**)

- John Ingham & Eleanor O'Brien – 16 Feb 1779 (Marriage, **St. Michan Parish (RC)**)

- John Ingham & Elizabeth Ellen Thulden

  o John Ingham Ingham – b. 15 May 1870, bapt. 18 Sep 1893 (Baptism, **St. Mary, Pro Cathedral Parish (RC)**)

John Ingham (father):

Residence - Manchester - September 18, 1893

- John Ingham & Isabel Cuthbert – 11 Oct 1716 (Marriage, **St. Nicholas Within Parish**)

- John Ingham & Jane Robinson, bur. 19 Nov 1777 (Burial, **St. Mark Parish**) – 4 Feb 1730 (Marriage, **St. Luke Parish**)

  o Diane Ingham – bapt. 16 Nov 1730 (Baptism, **St. Luke Parish**)

  o Anne Ingham – bapt. 12 Nov 1738 (Baptism, **St. Luke Parish**)

  o Mary Ingham – bapt. 9 Aug 1739 (Baptism, **St. Mark Parish**)

Ingham Surname Ireland: 1600s to 1900s

John Ingham (father):

Residence - St. John's Parish - February 4, 1730

Lazer's Hill - August 9, 1739

Jane Robinson (mother):

Residence - St. Luke's Parish - February 4, 1730

- John Ingham & Jean Ingham

  o Mary Ingham – bapt. 24 Jul 1737 (Baptism, **St. Catherine Parish**)

- John Ingham & Margaret Unknown

  o John Ingham – bapt. 8 Dec 1751 (Baptism, **St. James Parish**)

- John Ingham & Mary Borbidge – 10 Nov 1803 (Marriage, **St. Paul Parish**)

  o Flora Ingham – bapt. 17 Aug 1806 (Baptism, **St. Paul Parish**)

  o Mary Ingham – bapt. 26 May 1808 (Baptism, **St. Paul Parish**)

  o Charles Palmer Ingham – bapt. 10 Feb 1811 (Baptism, **St. Paul Parish**)

  o John Ingham – bapt. 28 Feb 1813 (Baptism, **St. Paul Parish**)

  o Rachel Ingham – bapt. 13 Nov 1814 (Baptism, **St. Paul Parish**)

- John Ingham & Mary Ingham

  o William Nelson Ingham – b. 6 May 1828, bapt. 28 May 1828 (Baptism, **Tralee Parish**)

- John Ingham & Mary Jocelyn – 22 Sep 1806 (Marriage, **St. Mary Parish**)

- John Ingham & Mary McCarthy

  o John Ingham – bapt. 1 Apr 1798 (Baptism, **Cork - South Parish** (RC))

Hurst

- John Ingham & Mary Unknown

  - William Ingham – bapt. 5 Apr 1702 (Baptism, **St. Nicholas Without Parish**)

John Ingham (father):

Residence - New Market - April 5, 1702

- John Ingham & Rose Fleetwood – 24 Aug 1709 (Marriage, **St. Michan Parish**)

John Ingham (husband):

Occupation - Footman - August 24, 1709

- John Ingham & Sarah Unknown

  - Elizabeth Mary Ingham – b. 2 Mar 1846, bapt. 30 Dec 1846 (Baptism, **St. Peter Parish**)

John Ingham (father):

Residence - Drumcondra - December 30, 1846

Occupation - Printer - December 30, 1846

- John Ingham & Susan Molloy – 28 Dec 1805 (Marriage, **St. Mary Parish**)
- John Ingham & Susan Unknown

  - Jane Ingham & James Burke – 8 Jan 1873 (Marriage, **St. Mary, Pro Cathedral Parish (RC)**)

Jane Ingham (daughter):

Residence - Fitzgibbon Street - January 8, 1873

James Burke, son of John Burke & Matilda Unknown (son-in-law):

Residence - London - January 8, 1873

- o Joseph Daniel Ingham & Monica Power – 27 Aug 1873 (Marriage, **St. Michan Parish (RC)**)

  - Josephine Mary Ingham – b. 2 Aug 1874, bapt. 6 Aug 1874 (Baptism, **St. Agatha Parish (RC)**)

  - Joseph August Ingham – b. 29 Aug 1875, bapt. 3 Sep 1875 (Baptism, **St. Agatha Parish (RC)**)

  - Susan Mary Elizabeth Ingham – b. 24 Feb 1877, bapt. 1 Mar 1877 (Baptism, **St. Agatha Parish (RC)**)

  - John Patrick Michael Ingham – b. 9 Jan 1882, bapt. 12 Jan 1882 (Baptism, **St. Agatha Parish (RC)**)

  - Francis De Sales Ingham – b. 2 Nov 1883, bapt. 6 Nov 1883 (Baptism, **St. Mary, Pro Cathedral Parish (RC)**)

  - William Aloysius Ingham – b. 26 Jun 1885, bapt. 2 Jul 1885 (Baptism, **St. Mary, Pro Cathedral Parish (RC)**)

  - Ignatius Mary Ingham – b. 17 Nov 1886, bapt. 23 Nov 1886 (Baptism, **St. Mary, Pro Cathedral Parish (RC)**)

  - Mary Veronica Ingham – b. 14 Jun 1889, bapt. 20 Jun 1889 (Baptism, **St. Mary, Pro Cathedral Parish (RC)**)

  - Claude May Leo Ingham – b. 25 Jun 1892, bapt. 2 Jul 1892 (Baptism, **St. Mary, Pro Cathedral Parish (RC)**)

Joseph Daniel Ingham (son):

Residence - 6 Fitzgibbon Street - August 27, 1873

2 Clonliffe Terrace - August 6, 1874

September 3, 1875

Hurst

March 1, 1877

January 12, 1882

49 Upper Gardiner Street - November 6, 1883

July 2, 1885

November 23, 1886

June 20, 1889

July 2, 1892

Monica Power, daughter of Patrick Power & Elizabeth Unknown (daughter-in-law):

Residence - 71 Eccles Street - August 27, 1873

- John Ingham & Unknown
  - Mary Ingham & William John Howard – 27 Feb 1882 (Marriage, **St. Anne Parish**)

Signatures:

Mary Ingham (daughter):

Residence - 16 Grafton Street - February 27, 1882

William John Howard, son of David Whiteside Howard & Unknown (son-in-law):

Residence - 14 Henry Street - February 27, 1882

Occupation - Draper - February 27, 1882

David Whiteside Howard (father):

Occupation - Hotel Keeper

John Ingham (father):

Occupation - Draper

Wedding Witnesses:

William Ingham & Susan Ingham

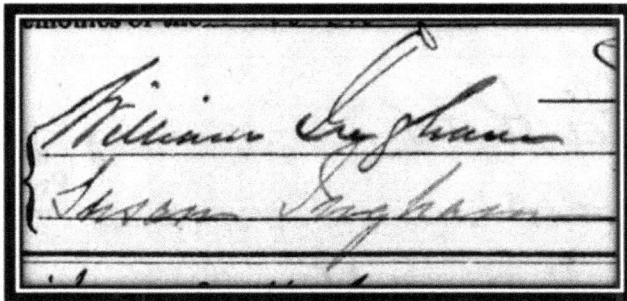

Signatures:

- Patrick Ingham & Margaret Finegan
  - James Joseph Ingham – b. 15 May 1896, bapt. 22 May 1896 (Baptism, **St. Mary, Pro Cathedral Parish** (RC))

Patrick Ingham (father):

Residence - 54 Great Britain Street - May 22, 1896

Hurst

- Patrick Ingham & Mary Croneen

  o Margaret Ingham – bapt. 6 Jan 1846 (Baptism, **Bantry Parish (RC)**)

- Richard Ingham & Anastasia Kane

  o Richard Ingham – b. 9 Oct 1869, bapt. 11 Oct 1869 (Baptism, **St. Nicholas Parish (RC)**)

Richard Ingham (father):

Residence - 38 Bride Street - October 11, 1869

- Richard Ingham & Anne Clinch – 9 Jan 1825 (Marriage, **St. Mary, Pro Cathedral Parish (RC)**)

  o Mary Ingham – bapt. 23 Nov 1826 (Baptism, **St. Mary, Pro Cathedral Parish (RC)**)

  o Margaret Ingham – bapt. 25 Nov 1827 (Baptism, **St. Mary, Pro Cathedral Parish (RC)**)

  o Anne Ingham – bapt. 20 Aug 1830 (Baptism, **St. Mary, Pro Cathedral Parish (RC)**)

  o Richard Ingham – bapt. 19 Sep 1834 (Baptism, **St. Mary, Pro Cathedral Parish (RC)**)

- Richard Ingham & Unknown

  o Margaret Ingham & Anthony Murray – 3 Sep 1855 (Marriage, **St. Mark Parish**)

Signatures:

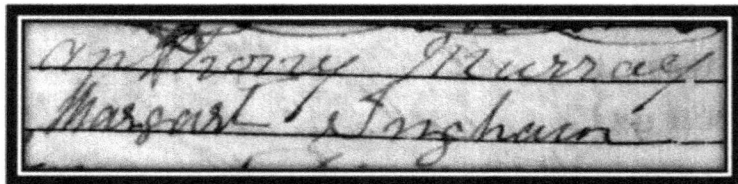
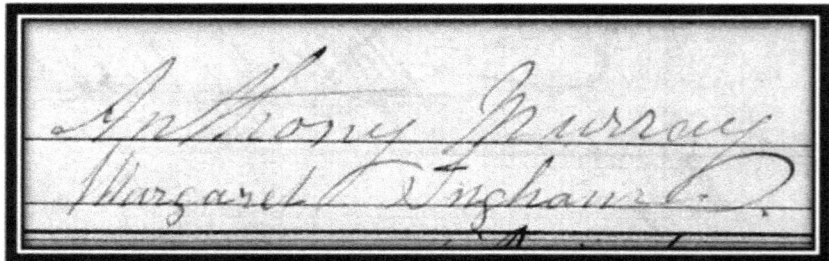

Ingham Surname Ireland: 1600s to 1900s

Margaret Ingham (daughter):

    Residence - 26 Cumberland Street South - September 3, 1855

Anthony Murray, son of Daniel Murray & Unknown (son-in-law):

    Residence - 26 Lincoln Place - September 3, 1855

    Occupation - Engineer - September 3, 1855

    Relationship Status - widow

Daniel Murray (father):

    Occupation - Gentleman Farmer

Richard Ingham (father):

    Occupation - Chandler

Wedding Witnesses:

James Duncan & Mary Duncan

Signatures:

Hurst

- Richard Clonmell Ingham & Anne Unknown

  - Catherine Ingham & Charles Quinn – 7 Jan 1859 (Marriage, **St. Catherine Parish** (RC))

    - Margaret Elizabeth Quinn – b. 18 Apr 1866, bapt. 30 Apr 1866 (Baptism, **St. Mary, Pro Cathedral Parish** (RC))

    - Frances Mary Quinn – b. 2 Aug 1868, bapt. 3 Aug 1868 (Baptism, **St. Mary, Pro Cathedral Parish** (RC))

    - Michael Joseph Quinn – b. 13 Aug 1871, bapt. 16 Aug 1871 (Baptism, **St. Mary, Pro Cathedral Parish** (RC))

Charles Quinn, son of Charles Quinn & Anne Unknown (son-in-law):

Residence - Clontarf - January 7, 1859

8 Elephant Lane - April 30, 1866

August 3, 1868

August 16, 1871

  - Anne Ingham & Elias Quinn – 21 Feb 1860 (Marriage, **St. Catherine Parish** (RC))

    - Michael Joseph Quinn – b. 20 May 1861, bapt. 24 May 1861 (Baptism, **St. Catherine Parish** (RC))

    - Margaret Mary Quinn – b. 30 Nov 1864, bapt. 6 Dec 1864 (Baptism, **St. Catherine Parish** (RC))

Anne Ingham (daughter):

- **Residence - 45 Meath Street - February 21, 1860**

Ingham Surname Ireland: 1600s to 1900s

Elias Quinn, son of Charles Quinn & Anne Unknown (son-in-law):

Residence - Clontarf - February 21, 1860

45 Meath Street - May 24, 1861

December 6, 1864

- Richard Patrick Ingham & Julia Mary Teresa Knight
    - Mary Helen Teresa Ingham – b. 1897, bapt. 1897 (Baptism, **St. Andrew Parish (RC)**)
    - Richard Henry Joseph Ingham – b. 1898, bapt. 1898 (Baptism, **St. Andrew Parish (RC)**)

Richard Patrick Ingham (father):

Residence - 11 Upper Mount Street - 1897

1898

- Robert Ingham & Alice Frezer – 14 Dec 1740 (Marriage, **St. Audoen Parish**)
- Robert Ingham & Mary Collice – 16 Dec 1722 (Marriage, **St. Bride Parish**)
- Unknown Ingham & Harriet Ingham – b. 1845, bur. 28 Sep 1874 (Burial, **Arbour Hill Barracks Parish**)

Unknown Ingham (husband):

Occupation - Captain 44th Regiment - September 28, 1874

Harriet Ingham (wife):

Residence - Dublin - September 28, 1874

- Unknown Ingham & Unknown

  o J. Cunliffe Ingham

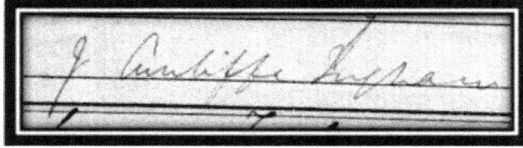

Signature:

- William Ingham & Anne Moore

  o John Ingham – bapt. 10 Oct 1836 (Baptism, **St. James Parish (RC)**)

- William Ingham & Anne Unknown

  o Margaret Ingham – bapt. 28 May 1734 (Baptism, **St. John Parish**)

- William Ingham & Anne Unknown

  o Thomas Ingham – b. 11 Aug 1817, bapt. 24 Aug 1817 (Baptism, **St. Peter Parish**)

- William Ingham & Jane Ingham

  o Thomas Ingham – bapt. 13 Nov 1853 (Baptism, **Arbour Hill Barracks Parish**)

William Ingham (father):

Residence - Royal Barracks - November 13, 1853

Occupation - Private 46 - November 13, 1853

- William Ingham & Leticia Baird

  o Sarah Christine Ingham – b. 1862, bapt. 1863 (Baptism, **St. Andrew Parish (RC)**)

William Ingham (father):

Residence - 9 James Place - 1863

Ingham Surname Ireland: 1600s to 1900s

- William Ingham & Sarah Unknown

  o John Ingham – bapt. 9 Feb 1779 (Baptism, **St. Catherine Parish**)

William Ingham (father):

Residence - Marrow Bone Lane - February 9, 1779

- William Ingham & Unknown

  o Sarah Jane Ingham & Thomas Roker – 4 Jun 1860 (Marriage, **St. Peter Parish**)

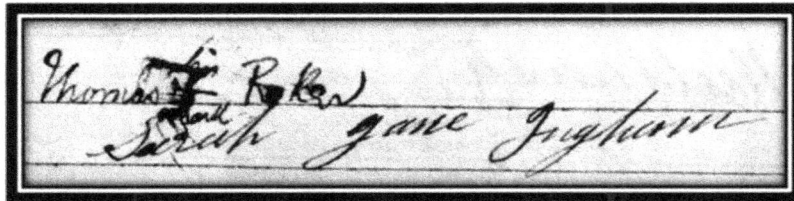

Signatures:

Sarah Jane Ingham (daughter):

Residence - 26 Percy Place - June 4, 1860

Thomas Roker, son of Thomas Roker & Unknown (son-in-law):

Residence - Portobello Barracks - June 4, 1860

Occupation - Driver Royal Artillery - June 4, 1860

Thomas Roker (father):

Occupation - Laborer

William Ingham (father):

Occupation - Sawyer

Hurst

Wedding Witnesses:

John Graham & Ellen Graham

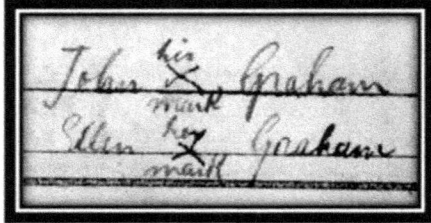

Signatures:

Individual Births/Baptisms

None were Listed

Individual Burials

- Agnes Ingham – bur. 7 Mar 1732 (Burial, **St. John Parish**)

- Florence Ingham – b. 1776, d. 3 Jan 1849, bur. 6 Jan 1849 (Burial, **Clontarf Parish**)

Florence Ingham (deceased):

> **Residence - Dublin - January 3, 1849**

> **Age at Death - 73 years**

- Catherine Ingham – b. 1801, bur. 25 Jan 1834 (Burial, **St. George Parish**)

Catherine Ingham (deceased):

> **Residence - Whitworth Hospital - before January 25, 1834**

> **Age at Death - 33 years**

- Dominick Ingham – bur. 7 Mar 1714 (Burial, **St. Nicholas Without Parish**)

Dominick Ingham (deceased):

> **Residence - New Market - before March 7, 1714**

- Endy Ingham – bur. 22 Feb 1812 (Burial, **St. Paul Parish**)

- Farmer Ingham – bur. 9 Sep 1813 (Burial, **St. Paul Parish**)

- George Ingham – b. 1758, bur. 12 Oct 1837 (Burial, **St. Catherine Parish**)

Ingham Surname Ireland: 1600s to 1900s

George Ingham (deceased):

    Residence - Meath Street - before October 12, 1837

    Age at Death - 79 years

    Cause of Death - old age

- George Ingham – b. 1778, d. 13 Jan 1855, bur. 15 Jan 1855 (Burial, **Clontarf Parish**)

George Ingham (deceased):

    Residence - Clontarf - January 13, 1855

    Age at Death - 77 years

- George Ingham – b. 1834, bur. 13 May 1864 (Burial, **Clontarf Parish**)

George Ingham (deceased):

    Residence - Clontarf - Before May 13, 1864

    Age at Death - 30 years

- Jane Ingham – bur. 4 Apr 1812 (Burial, **St. Mary Parish**)

Jane Ingham (deceased):

    Residence - Jervis Street - before April 4, 1812

- John Ingham – bur. 30 May 1704 (Burial, **St. Peter Parish**)

John Ingham (deceased):

    Residence - White Friar Lane - before May 30, 1704

Hurst

- John Ingham – bur. 20 Feb 1730 (Burial, **St. Nicholas Without Parish**)

John Ingham (deceased):

Residence - Coombe - before February 20, 1730

- John Ingham – bur. 23 Sep 1800 (Burial, **St. Paul Parish**)
- John Ingham – bur. 13 Jul 1827 (Burial, **St. Paul Parish**)
- John Ingham – bur. 2 Jun 1843 (Burial, **St. Paul Parish**)

John Ingham (deceased):

Residence - Royal Infirmary - before June 2, 1843

Occupation - Private 2nd Dragoon Guards - before June 2, 1843

- Martha Ingham – bur. Feb 1711 (Burial, **St. Nicholas Without Parish**)

Martha Ingham (deceased):

Residence - New Market - Before February 1711

- Mary Magdalena Ingham – bur. 2 Oct 1838 (Burial, **St. Paul Parish**)
- Thomas Ingham – b. 1820, bur. 16 Nov 1837 (Burial, **St. Mark Parish**)

Thomas Ingham (deceased):

Residence - George's Quay - before November 16, 1837

Age at Death - 17 years

- Unknown Ingham – bur. 23 Dec 1700 (Burial, **St. Nicholas Without Parish**)

Ingham Surname Ireland: 1600s to 1900s

Unknown Ingham (deceased):

> **Residence - New Market - before December 23, 1700**

> **Occupation - Church Warden - before December 23, 1700**

- Unknown Ingham – bur. 29 Oct 1717 (Burial, **St. Nicholas Without Parish**)

Unknown Ingham (deceased):

> **Residence - St. Luke Parish - before October 29, 1717**

> **Relationship Status - widow**

- Unknown Ingham – bur. 6 Feb 1730 (Burial, **St. Nicholas Without Parish**)

Unknown Ingham (deceased):

> **Residence - St. Catherine's Parish - before February 6, 1730**

- Unknown Ingham – bur. 12 Aug 1731 (Burial, **St. Nicholas Without Parish**)

Unknown Ingham (deceased):

> **Residence - St. Catherine's Parish - before August 12, 1731**

- Unknown Ingham – bur. 13 Mar 1732 (Burial, **St. Nicholas Without Parish**)

Unknown Ingham (deceased):

> **Residence - St. Luke's Parish - before March 13, 1732**

- Unknown Ingham – bur. 19 Jun 1744 (Burial, **St. Nicholas Without Parish**)
- Unknown Ingham (Child) – bur. 30 Aug 1786 (Burial, **St. Mary Parish**)

Hurst

Unknown Ingham (Child):

Place of Burial - Mary's Abby - August 30, 1786

- Unknown Ingham (Mrs.) – b. 1800, bur. 11 May 1872 (Burial, **Clontarf Parish**)

Unknown Ingham (Mrs.) (deceased):

Residence - Formerly Clontarf - Before May 11, 1872

Age at Death - 72 years

- William Ingham (Child) – bur. 2 Apr 1749 (Burial, **St. Paul Parish**)

- William Ingham – bur. 4 Oct 1804 (Burial, **St. Paul Parish**)

Individual Marriages

- Anne Ingham & Richard King

  o Elizabeth King – b. 22 Dec 1863, bapt. 30 Dec 1863 (Baptism, **St. Agatha Parish** (RC))

  o John Joseph King – b. 23 May 1869, bapt. 24 May 1869 (Baptism, **St. Michan Parish** (RC))

Richard King (father):

Residence - Quinn's Place - December 30, 1863

8 Dorset Row - May 24, 1869

- Bridget Ingham & James Dillon Meldon – 30 Nov 1832 (Marriage, **St. Mary, Pro Cathedral Parish** (RC))

  o James Felix Meldon – bapt. 30 May 1837 (Baptism, **St. Mary, Pro Cathedral Parish** (RC))

  o Augustine Meldon, bapt. 1843 (Baptism, **St. Mary Parish** (RC)) & Catherine Pugin – 15 Jul 1871 (Marriage, **Harrington Street Parish** (RC))

Augustine Meldon (son):

Residence - Westland Row - July 15, 1871

Catherine Pugin, daughter of August W. Pugin & Louisa Barton (daughter-in-law):

Residence - 90 Stephen's Green South - July 15, 1871

  o Albert Meldon – bapt. 1845 (Baptism, **St. Mary Parish** (RC))

  o Bridget Meldon – bapt. 1847 (Baptism, **St. Mary Parish** (RC))

Hurst

o   Josephine Mary Meldon, bapt. 1849 (Baptism, **St. Mary Parish (RC)**) & Raymond Carroll – 6 Oct 1879 (Marriage, **St. Mary, Donnybrook Parish (RC)**)

Josephine Mary Meldon (daughter):

Residence - Casino - October 6, 1879

Raymond Carroll, son of Raymond Carroll & Helen Taaffe (son-in-law):

Residence - 2 Great Denmark Street - October 6, 1879

o   Lewis Meldon & Rose Mary Kenny – 8 Jun 1881 (Marriage, **St. Mary, Donnybrook Parish (RC)**)

Lewis Meldon (son):

Residence - Merrion Square Street - June 8, 1881

Rose Mary Kenny, daughter of George Kenny & Mary Anne Unknown

(daughter-in-law):

Residence - Ailesbury Road - June 8, 1881

o   Joseph Meldon & Helen Pennefather – 29 Aug 1887 (Marriage, **St. Mary, Pro Cathedral Parish (RC)**)

Joseph Meldon (son):

Residence - 24 Merrion Square - August 29, 1887

Helen Pennefather, daughter of William Pennefather & Catherine Scott

(daughter-in-law):

Residence - 4 Mount Joy Place - August 29, 1887

Ingham Surname Ireland: 1600s to 1900s

- Caroline Ingham & John Daly – 13 May 1847 (Marriage, **St. Mary, Pro Cathedral Parish (RC)**)

- Eleanor Ingham & Michael Murphy

  - Michael Murphy – bapt. 28 Feb 1820 (Baptism, **SS. Michael & John Parish (RC)**)

  - John Murphy – bapt. 6 May 1822 (Baptism, **SS. Michael & John Parish (RC)**)

  - Henry Murphy – bapt. 7 Nov 1824 (Baptism, **SS. Michael & John Parish (RC)**)

- Florence Ingham & Thomas Whelan

  - Thomas Whelan & Catherine Moore – 26 Aug 1883 (Marriage, **St. Mary, Pro Cathedral Parish (RC)**)

Thomas Whelan (son):

Residence - 3 Russell Cottages - August 26, 1883

Catherine Moore, daughter of William Moore & Alice McAuley (daughter-in-law):

Residence - 4 Rutland Place - August 26, 1883

  - Florence Whelan & John Flynn – 9 May 1886 (Marriage, **St. Mary, Pro Cathedral Parish (RC)**)

Florence Whelan (daughter):

Residence - 1 Russell Cottages - May 9, 1886

John Flynn, son of William Flynn & Anne O' Connor (son-in-law):

Residence - 5 Kane's Court - May 9, 1886

Hurst

- o Lawrence Whelan & Ellen Shannon – 22 Sep 1889 (Marriage, **St. Mary, Pro Cathedral Parish** (RC))

Lawrence Whelan (son):

Residence - 115 Gloucester Street - September 22, 1889

Ellen Shannon, daughter of Dennis Shannon & Mary Connor (daughter-in-law):

Residence - 18 Mabbot Street - September 22, 1889

- o Henry Ignatius Whelan – b. 11 Jan 1870, bapt. 17 Jan 1870 (Baptism, **St. Michan Parish** (RC))

Thomas Whelan (father):

Residence - 74 Lower Dorset Street - January 17, 1870

- • Harriet Ingham & James Adams
  - o Catherine Adams, bapt. 9 Feb 1823 (Baptism, **SS. Michael & John Parish** (RC)) & Peter John Dermody (D e r m o d y) – 15 Feb 1857 (Marriage, **St. Catherine Parish** (RC))

Catherine Adams (daughter):

Residence - 1 New Row - February 15, 1857

Peter John Dermody (D e r m o d y), son of Patrick Dermody (D e r m o d y) & Sarah Gernon (G e r n o n) (son-in-law):

Residence - Vagus - February 15, 1857

- o Mary Anne Adams – bapt. 20 Mar 1825 (Baptism, **SS. Michael & John Parish** (RC))

Ingham Surname Ireland: 1600s to 1900s

- Horice Ingham & Michael Croneen – 28 Feb 1832 (Marriage, **Bantry Parish** (RC))

- Mary Ingham & Jeremiah Anderson

  - John Francis Anderson – bapt. 1864 (Baptism, **St. Mary Parish** (RC))

- Mary Ingham & Joseph Blundell – 17 Feb 1748 (Marriage, **St. Bride Parish**)

Joseph Blundell (husband):

Occupation - Merchant

- Mary Ellen Ingham & John Stewart Stevenson

  - Josephine Maude Jane Stevenson – b. 1876, bapt. 1876 (Baptism, **St. Mary Parish** (RC))

  - Louisa Mary Stevenson – b. 18 Nov 1877, bapt. 26 Nov 1877 (Baptism, **St. Mary, Donnybrook Parish** (RC))

John Stewart Stevenson (father):

Residence - Upper Leeson Street - November 26, 1877

- Sarah Ingham & Edward Lawlor – 12 Jan 1787 (Marriage, **St. Andrew Parish** (RC))

- Sarah Ingham & Meei Firth – 13 Apr 1722 (Marriage, **St. Nicholas Within Parish**)

- Unknown Ingham & Samuel Morgan – 3 Oct 1746 (Marriage, **St. Audoen Parish**)

Unknown Ingham (wife):

Residence - Back Lane - October 3, 1746

Relationship Status - widow

Name Variations

Includes Latin and Abbreviated forms of names found in the original documents.

Abigail = Abigale, Abigall

Anne = Ann, Anna, Annae

Bartholomew = Barth, Bartholmeus, Bartholomeo

Bridget = Birgis, Brigid, Brigida, Bridgit

Catherine = Catharine, Catharina, Catharinae, Catherina, Cath, Catha, Cathae, Cathe, Cathn, Kate

Charles = Carolus, Charls, Chas

Christopher = Christoph

Daniel = Danielem, Danielis

Edmund = Edmond

Edward = Ed, Edwd

Eleanor = Eleo, Eleonora, Elinor, Ellenor

Elizabeth = Betty, Elisa, Elisabeth, Eliz, Eliza, Elizab, Elizh, Elizth

Ellen = Elena, Ellena

Emily = Emilia

Esther = Essie, Ester

Francis = Fransicum

George = Geo, Georg, Georgius

Grace = Gratiae

Gulielmo = Guil, Guillelmi, Gulielmum, Guillelmus, Gulmi

Harold = Harry

Ingham Surname Ireland: 1600s to 1900s

Helen = Helena

Honor = Hanora, Honora

James = Jacobi, Jacobus, Jas

Jane = Joanna

Jeanne = Jeannae, Joannae

Joan = Johanna, Joney

John = Jno, Joannem, Joannes, Johannis

Joseph = Jos

Juliana = Julian

Leticia = Letitia, Lettice, Letticia

Lewis = Louis

Luke = Lucas

Margaret = Margarita, Margaritae, Margeret, Marget, Margt

Martha = Marthae

Mary = Maria, My

Mary Anne = Marianna, Marianne, Maryanne

Michael = Michaelis, Michl

Patrick = Pat, Patt, Patk, Patricii, Patricius

Peter = Petri

Richard = Ricardi, Ricardus, Rich, Richd

Robert = Roberti

Rose = Rosa, Rosae

Thomas = Thom, Thomae, Thoms, Thos, Ths

Timothy = Timotheus, Timy

William = Wil, Will, Willm, Wm

Notes

Notes

Notes

Notes

Notes

Notes

Index

A

B

C

D

F

Hurst

Hurst

Ingham Surname Ireland: 1600s to 1900s

About The Author

Donovan Hurst graduated from San Diego State University with a Bachelor of Arts in the major field of studies of History and a minor in the field of studies of Anthropology. He is a current member of The General Society of Mayflower Descendants and has been conducting genealogical research for over 10 years tracing back his ancestors to their ancestral homelands in Denmark, England, France, Germany, Ireland, Norway, and Scotland.

www.ingramcontent.com/pod-product-compliance
Lightning Source LLC
Chambersburg PA
CBHW081203270326
41930CB00014B/3283